A Narrative of the Life of Rev. Noah Davis

REV. NOAH DAVIS,
PASTOR OF THE
Saratoga Street African Baptist Church,
BALTIMORE.

A Narrative of the Life of Rev. Noah Davis

NOTICE TO THE PUBLIC.

THE object of the writer, in preparing this account of himself, is to

RAISE SUFFICIENT MEANS TO FREE HIS LAST TWO CHILDREN FROM SLAVERY.

Having already, within twelve years past, purchased himself, his wife, and five of his children, at a cost, altogether, of over four thousand dollars, he now earnestly desires a humane and Christian public to

AID HIM IN THE SALE OF THIS BOOK,

for the purpose of finishing the task in which he has so long and anxiously labored.

God has blessed him in an extraordinary manner, not only by granting freedom to him and so large a portion of his family, but by giving him the hope of the gospel, and permitting him to preach that gospel among his own people--in which calling he has been engaged for about twenty-five years.

The Life of Rev. Noah Davis
A Narrative of a Colored Man.
Written By Himself, at the Age of Fifty-Four

By

Rev. Noah Davis

THE SARATOGA STREET

AFRICAN BAPTIST CHAPEL.

The building, of which the above cut is an imperfect representation, fronts as above 100 feet on Saratoga street, and 46 feet on Calvert street. The house is of brick, and cost over $18,000.—(See page 45.)

AFRICAN BAPTIST CHAPEL.
The building, of which the above cut is an imperfect representation, fronts as above 100 feet on Saratoga street, and 46 feet on Calvert street. The house is of brick, and cost over $18,000

THE LIFE
OF
REV. NOAH DAVIS

A

NARRATIVE
OF
A COLORED MAN.
WRITTEN BY HIMSELF, AT THE AGE OF FIFTY-FOUR.

LARGE PRINT EDITION

PRINTED SOLELY FOR THE AUTHOR'S BENEFIT.

BALTIMORE:
PUBLISHED BY JOHN F. WEISHAMPEL, JR.,
No. 484 West Baltimore St.

STEREOTYPED BY
JOHN F. WEISHAMPEL, JR., BOOKSELLER
AND PUBLISHER,
BALTIMORE.

A Narrative of the Life of Rev. Noah Davis

CONTENTS.

A Narrative of the Life of
Rev. Noah Davis

NARRATIVE.
CHAPTER I.

Early Life in Virginia--Example of Pious Parents.

I WAS born a slave, in Madison county, Virginia, March, 1804. My father, John Davis, and his family, belonged to Robert Patten, Esq., a wealthy merchant, residing in Fredericksburg--who was also owner, in connection with Mr. John Thom, of a large merchant mill, located on "Crooked Run," a stream running between Madison and Culpepper counties. My father was the head miller in that large establishment, in which responsible station he was much respected.

There I was born, and remained until I was twelve years old. Mr. Patten was always considered one of the best of masters, allowing his servants many privileges; but my father enjoyed more than many others. Both he and my mother were pious members of a Baptist church, and from their godly example, I formed a determination, before I had reached my twelfth year, that if I was spared to become a man, I would try to be as good as my parents. My father could read a little, and make figures, but could scarcely write at all. His custom, on those Sabbaths when we remained at home, was to spend his time in instructing his children, or the neighboring servants, out of a New Testament, sent him from Fredericksburg by one of his older sons. I fancy I can see him now, sitting under his bush arbor, reading that precious book to many attentive hearers around him.

Such was the esteem I had for my pious father, that I have kept that blessed book ever since his death, for his sake; and it was the first New Testament I read, after I felt the pardoning love of God in my soul.

My father died, August 20, 1826, aged 60 years. My mother, Jane Davis, at the death of my father, removed from the farm, where my father died, and spent the remainder of her days in Fredericksburg, with her children. She lived to good old age, and fell asleep in Jesus, Dec. 24, 1831.

My father had been allowed to keep a cow and horse, for his own use; and to raise and feed his hogs and poultry from the mill.--He had the privilege of keeping his children with him, until they were old enough to put out to such trades as they might choose. I had several brothers and one sister. Two of my brothers, one older, the other younger than myself, lived with our parents, at this place. My oldest brother worked in the mill, with my father, while my youngest brother and I did little else than play about home, and wait upon our mother. I had several playmates, besides my brothers, and among them were the sons of Col. Thom, and the servant boys who stayed at his house. Although many years have passed away since, it gives me pleasure, even now, to recollect the happy seasons I enjoyed with the playmates of my childhood.

But this pleasant state of things was not to continue long. The owners of the mill and farm concluded to sell out the whole concern. My father and his family then removed to another farm, belonging to our owner, located in Culpeper county, near

Stevensburg. Here I remained nearly two years, working, part of the time, with a carpenter, who was building a summer residence for my master; and the rest of the time, assisting my father to cultivate as much ground as he and his family could tend. Here I learned something of a farmer's life. The overseer, Mr. Daniel Brown, had the reputation of being one of the best overseers in the county. But my father's family was not put under him further than for his protection; for after our owner sold the mill, he set my parents free, and allowed them to maintain themselves, by cultivating as much ground on the farm as they needed.

Sometimes my father would leave his little place in charge of my brother Robert and myself, and would hire himself to work in some mill, or go peddling poultry, vegetables, &c., at some of the market places around.

CHAPTER II.

Apprenticed to the shoe making--
Learns housework-- Intemperance--
"A negro can't be trusted"--Learning
how to write and cipher.

IN December, 1818, for the first time in
my life, I left my parents, to go a distance
from home; and I was sad at the thought of
parting with those whom I loved and
reverenced more than any persons on earth.
But the expectation of seeing
Fredericksburg, a place which, from all I
had then learned, I supposed must be the
greatest place in the world, reconciled me
somewhat with the necessity of saying
Good-bye to the dear ones at home. I arrived
at Fredericksburg, after a day and a half's
travel, in a wagon--a distance of some fifty
miles. Having arrived in town, a boy green
from the country, I was astonished and
delighted at what appeared to me the
splendor and beauty of the place. I spent a
merry Christmas at my old master's stately
mansion, along with my older brother, and
for a while forgot the home on the farm.

But soon, another home was selected for me, where I might learn a trade, and as I preferred the boot and shoe-making, I was put to Mr. Thomas Wright, a man of sterling integrity, who was considered the best workman in the whole town. Here I had an older brother living, which was some inducement for my going to live with Mr. Wright. I was bound, to serve until I should be twenty-one years old. This was in January, 1819.

Upon entering with Mr. Wright, I learned that the colored boys had to serve one year with Mrs. Wright, in the house and kitchen. The object of this was to train them for future usefulness, when called from the shop, to serve as waiters or cooks. Mrs. Wright was a good manager, and a very particular housekeeper. I used to think she was too particular. But I have learned better since. I have often wished, when I have been seeking homes for my children, that I could find one like Mrs. Wright. She would spare no pains to teach her servants how she wanted her work done; and then she would spare no pains to make them do it. I have often looked back, with feelings of gratitude and veneration, to that pious lady, for her untiring perseverance in training me up in the way I should go. But she is gone, as I trust, to receive the reward of righteousness, in a better world.

After I had been under Mrs. Wright's special charge the first year, she could leave me to cook a dinner, or clean the house, or do anything she might set me at, without her being present. I was now considered fit to take my seat among the hands in the shop.

Here I found quite a new state of things. The shoemakers, at that time, in Fredericksburg were considered the most intemperate of any class of men in the place; and as the apprentice-boys had always to be very obliging to the journeymen, in order to get along pleasantly with them, it was my duty to be runner for the shop; and I was soon trained how to bring liquor among the men with such secrecy as to prevent the boss, who had forbidden it to come on the premises, from knowing it.

But, in those days, the drinking of ardent spirits was a common practice, even among Christians. With such examples all around, I soon learned the habit of drinking, along with every other vile habit to which my companions were addicted. It was true in my case, that "evil communications corrupt good manners;" and had it not been for the strictness with which my boss and his amiable lady watched over me, I should in all probability have become a confirmed drunkard, before my time was out. But they held the reins over me, and kept me in, until I had served out my apprenticeship.

I can say, however, that, much as I was inclined to other vices and sins, Mr. Wright readily gave me a recommendation for honesty, truthfulness, and goodness of character. In fact, he had felt such confidence in me, that he would often leave his shoe store in my care, when he would have to go to the north, for a supply of stock. And I can truly say, that I never deceived him, when he thus trusted me. Nothing would mortify me as much, as to hear it said, "A negro can't be trusted." This saying would always nerve me with a determination to be trustworthy.-- If I was trusted, I would deserve to be trusted. I wanted to show that principle was not confined to color. But I have been led to look at it since, and have thought that perhaps it was more pride than principle in me, at that time, for I was a wicked sinner.

The first idea I ever got of writing, was from trying to imitate my employer, who used to write the names of his customers on the lining of the boots and shoes, as he gave them out to be made. So I tried to make letters, and soon succeeded in writing my name, and then the word Fredericksburg, and so on. My father had previously taught me the alphabet, in the spelling book, before I had left the mill. After I became religious, I would carry my father's New Testament to church, and always try to get to meeting in time to hear the preacher read a chapter before sermon. If he named the chapter before reading it, I would soon find it. In this way, I gathered much information in pronouncing many hard words in the Scriptures.

It was a long time before I learned the meaning of the numeral letters put in the Bible over the chapters. I had often seen them in the spelling book running alongside a column of figures; but no one ever told me that they were put there for the same use as the figures.

CHAPTER III.

Religious Experience--Conviction--
Conversion.

Just about the close of my apprenticeship, and as I began to feel myself a man, I commenced to visit the girls, which induced me go still more frequently to church.

At that time, there were four churches in Fredericksburg. The colored people had apartments for worship with the white people, at each of these churches. They were Methodist, Presbyterian, Episcopalian and Baptist.

I had no particular preference for any one of these denominations, more than another; but, went wherever my favorites went. One night a young lady invited me to go to the Methodist church, where a prayer meeting was to be held. During the meeting, a venerable old gentleman rose to his feet, and related an account of the sudden death of a young lady, which he had read in a newspaper. When he related that solemn circumstance, it so affected me, that I felt as if I was about to die, in a sudden manner also.

Having always, from parental training, purposed in my mind to become religious before I died, I thought that now was the time to begin to pray. But I could not try to pray in the church, for I was afraid that the girls would laugh at me. Yet I became so troubled, that I left the house, girls and all, intending to seek some place where I might pray. But to my horror and surprise, when I got out of the church, this reflection occurred to me, "God is in heaven, and you are on earth:--how can He hear you?" O, what distress of mind I now felt! I began to wonder how God could hear my prayer;. for, sure enough, He was in heaven, and I on the earth. In my perplexity, I started for home.

Just before I reached the shop, where I slept, this thought struck me, if possible with more force than the former reflection: "God does see you!" It really appeared to me as if I could see that God was indeed looking at me; and not only so, but I felt that He had been looking at me all my life. I now said to myself, "It is of no use for me to pray.-- If God has seen all my wickedness, as I feel that He has, then there is no mercy for me."

So I ran to my lodging-place, and tried to hide myself in a dark room. But this was useless; for it appeared that God could see me in the dark, as well as in the light.

I now felt constrained to beg for mercy, and spent the time in trying to obtain pardon for my sins. But the morning came, and the hour drew near for the hands to go to work, and I was still unhappy.

I felt so very different to what I had always felt, that I tried to examine my impressions of the previous night, to learn if it was true that God did see me or not; for I thought my imagination might have deceived me.

Up to this time, I was not fully convinced that God knew all about me. So I began to study about the matter. As I sat on the shoe-bench, I picked up a bunch of bristles, and selecting one of the smallest, I began to wonder, if God could see an object so small as that. No sooner had this inquiry arose in my heart, than it appeared to me, that the Lord could not only see the bristle, but that He beheld me, as, plainly as I saw the little object in my hand; and not only so, but that God was then looking through me, just as I would hold up a tumbler of clear water to the sun and look through it. This was enough. I felt that I must pray, or perish; and now I began to pray.

But it really seemed, that the more I prayed the less hope there was for me. Still I could not stop praying; for I felt that God was angry with me. I had sinned against his holy laws; and now, if He should cut me off, and send me to hell, it was but right. These thoughts followed me day and night, for five weeks, before I felt relief. At length, one day, while sitting on my shoe bench, I felt that my time had come when I must die. What troubled me most, was that I should have to appear before God, in all my sins;-- O, what horror filled my soul at the thought!

I began to wonder what I must do. I knew I was not prepared for death and the Judgment. It is true that two of my shopmates, at that time, were members of the church; but they did not seem to care for my soul. All the rest of the hands were as wicked as myself. "What shall I do?" was in my mind, all the time I sat at work.

The reflection occurred to me, "Your mother is a Christian; it may be she can save you." But this suggestion appeared to be offensive to God. Then came another thought,--"As my master was a rich man, could he not do something to help me?" But I found no relief in either . . . . and while I sat thus, hoping and praying, light broke into my mind--all my trouble left me in an instant.

I felt such a love and peace flowing in my soul, that I could not sit longer; I sprang to my feet, and cried out, "Glory to God!" It seemed to me, that God, whom I had beheld, a few seconds previously, angry with me, was now well pleased. I could not tell why this great change had taken place in me; and my shopmates were surprised at my conduct, saying, that I must be getting crazy. But, just at this moment, the thought came into my mind, that I was converted; still, as I felt so very different from what I had expected to feel, I could not see how that could be. I concluded to run and see my mother, and ask her how people felt, when they got converted. So I went, right away, to my mother's house, some five or six squares from the shop.

When I reached the door of her house, it appeared to me that everything was new and bright. I went in, and sat down. Mother asked me how I was. I told her, I felt right smart. This was a new sound from me; for my answers to this question had long been-- "poorly." But now came the trial; to ask mother how people felt, when they were converted. I felt ashamed to ask the question; so I went into another room; and seeing a hymnbook lying on the table, I took it up. The first hymn that struck my sight began with these words:

"When converts first begin to sing,
Their happy souls are on the wing--
Their theme is all redeeming love;
Fain would they be with Christ above.

With admiration they behold
The love of Christ, which can't be told,"
&c.

These lines expressed my feelings precisely, and being encouraged from them, I went to my mother, and asked her the question-- "How do people feel, when they get converted?" She replied, "Do you think you are converted?" Now, this was a severe trial; for, although I felt that I was really changed, yet I wanted to hear from her, before I could decide whether I was actually converted, or not. I replied, "No." Then she said, "My son, the devil makes people think themselves converted, sometimes." I arose, and left immediately, believing that the devil had made a fool of me. I returned to my shop, more determined to pray than ever before.

I arrived, and took my seat, and tried to get under that same weight, that I had felt pressing me down, but a short while before. But it seemed to me that I could not; and, instead of feeling sad, I felt joyful in my heart; and while trying to pray, I thought the Savior appeared to me. I thought I saw God smiling upon me, through Christ, His Son. My soul was filled with love to God and Jesus Christ. It appeared to me, I saw a fullness in Jesus Christ, to save every sinner who would come to Him. And I felt, that if I was only converted, I would tell all sinners how precious the Savior was. But I could not think myself converted yet, because I could not see what I had done, for God to pardon my sins. Still I felt a love to Him for what He had done for my soul.

Then I began to think upon my shopmates --and, O what pity ran through my soul for them. I wished to pray for them; but I felt so unworthy, that I could not do it. At last, I promised the Lord that if He would convert my soul, I would talk to them.

* * It was several months after that, before I was made to realize this to be the work of God; and when it was made plain, O what joy it did bring to my poor soul!

I shortly became a member of the Baptist church, and was baptized, in company with some twenty others, by Rev. Geo. F. Adams, who was then pastor of the Baptist church in Fredericksburg-- September 19,1831. This then contained about three hundred colored members.

CHAPTER IV.

Marriage--License to Preach--Purchase of
Freedom--A Call to Baltimore.

I HAD not been a member of the
church a great while, before I formed an
attachment to a young woman, who
ultimately became my wife. I have ever
regarded her as the special gift of God to
me. She embraced religion about the same
time that I did. We had been acquainted with
each other for several years previous, and
although we associated frequently in the
same social circle together; yet nothing of a
special liking had manifested itself until the
day she was baptized.

But we were both slaves, and of course
had to get the consent of our owners, before
we went further. My wife belonged to the
late Carter L. Stephenson, Esq., who was a
brother to Hon. Andrew Stephenson, of Va.
My wife's master was quite indulgent to the
servants about the house. He never
restrained visitors from coming on his
premises to visit his domestics. It was said
he had the likeliest set of servant girls in the

town; and though I cannot say I got the prettiest, yet I think I got the best one among them. We have lived happily together, as husband and wife, for the last twenty-eight years. We have had nine children--seven born in slavery, and two since my wife's freedom. Five out of the seven in slavery I have bought--two are still in bondage.

Before long, the brethren chose me to fill the office of a deacon. But it never seemed to me to be the place that God designed for me; though I felt willing to do whatever lay in my power for God's glory and the good of His people. The impression made upon my at my conversion, to talk to sinners, increased on me, until I could wait no longer.

I related my convictions of duty to my brethren, and particularly to one who was always held in high esteem for his piety and excellent character--a colored brother, Armistead Walker. My case was first brought by him before the colored portion of the church; and after a full hearing of my statement, by the white brethren, with regard to my call to preach, &c., I was licensed to preach the gospel, and exhort sinners to repentance, opportunity might be afforded. I had ample opportunities at that time, for doing good, by preaching to my fellow men, both in town and country.

Several other colored brethren, about this time, gave evidence of having been called of God, to the work of preaching the gospel. Among these was a dear brother, named Alexander Daniel. He was a bright and shining light, among our people, and everything considered, I think he was the best preacher of color I ever heard. But alas, he is no more! He was esteemed as a Christian minister, and his friends, both white and colored, united in erecting a monument over his grave.

In my attempts to preach the gospel to my fellow sinners, I often felt embarrassed, not knowing how to read a chapter in the Bible correctly. My desires now increased for such a knowledge of the sacred Scriptures, as would enable me to read a chapter publicly to my hearers. I thought that if I had all my time at my own command, I would devote it all to divine things. This desire I think, led me more than anything else, to ask permission of my master, Dr. F. Patten, to purchase my freedom. I made this a subject of prayer, both night and day, that God would show me what he would have me do. I felt encouraged to hope that I should find favor with my owner, as he had always treated me kindly. But how shall I get the purchase money, provided he grants my request?-- This appeared a difficult matter, but I thought if my master would give me a chance, that I should be able to raise the money.

I went to him and stated my wishes, informing him why I wanted to be free--that I had been led to believe the Lord had converted my soul, and had called me to talk to sinners. He granted my request, without a single objection, fixing my price at five hundred dollars.

But now I had to tell him that I had no Money, and that I desired him to grant me another request; which was, to let me travel and find friends, who would give me the money. After learning my wishes fully, he consented, and told me, when I got ready to start, he would give me a pass, to go where I pleased.

I thanked him sincerely for this privilege, and after making arrangements, in the way of obtaining suitable letters of recommendation, I left Fredericksburg, in June, 1845, for Philadelphia, New York, Boston, &c.

After spending nearly four months in visiting the northern cities, I returned home, with about one hundred and fifty dollars, greatly disheartened.

Previous to going north, I had raised about a hundred and fifty dollars, which I had already paid on my debt.

The cause of my failure to raise all the money, I believe, was that I was unaccustomed to addressing large congregations of strangers; and often, when I was favored with an opportunity of presenting my case to the people, I would feel such embarrassment that I could scarcely say anything. And I met another obstacle, which discouraged me very much; which was, that some persons would tell me they sympathized with me, in my efforts to get free; but they said it was against their principles to give money, to buy slaves. I confess, this was new to me, and would cut me down much in my spirits--still I found generous and noble-hearted friends, who treated me with every mark of kindness.

I began to wonder to myself, whether God was in this matter, or not; and if so, why I had not succeeded. However, having returned home, I went to work at my trade, for the purpose of earning the remainder of the money. Having paid what I was able, toward my debt, and reserving enough to open a shop, upon my own account, my old boss, Mr. Wright, my true and constant friend, became my protector, so that I might carry on my business lawfully. In this, however, I was not very successful; but I had not been long engaged at it, before I received a communication from my white

Baptist friends in Baltimore, through my pastor, Rev. Sam'l Smith, informing me that if I would come to Baltimore, and accept an appointment as missionary to the colored people of that city, they would assist me in raising the balance of the money then due upon myself.

This was indeed an unexpected, and to me an undesired call. I began to think, how can I leave my wife and seven small children, to go to Baltimore to live, a distance of more than a hundred miles from them. This, I thought, could not be. I thought my children would need my watchful care, more now than at any other time. It is true, they were all slaves, belonging to a rich widow lady. But she had always given me the entire control of my family. Now, if I should leave them at their tender age, mischief might befall them. Still, as the letter from Baltimore was from gentlemen of the best standing, it became me to give them an answer. This I could not do, without first consulting my master. I did so, and after giving the matter a careful consideration, he thought I had better go and see those gentlemen--he was perfectly willing to leave the matter to me.

The result was, that I accepted the offer of the brethren in Baltimore; and by them, I was enabled to pay the debt I owed; and I have never had cause to repent it--though I had misgivings sometimes, when I would get into trouble.

But I have found those who were my friends at first, are my friends still. In a few weeks after I had arrived in Baltimore, (1847,) the white Baptists who were favorable to the mission in behalf of the colored people, secured for me an appointment as missionary of the Domestic Board of the Southern Baptist Convention, in connection with the Maryland Baptist Union Association. I now felt a debt of gratitude to these dear friends, that I could not show more acceptably to them, than by engaging heartily in the work to which I had been thus called. I went to work, first, by hiring a room in a private house, where I would collect what few children I could get together, in a Sabbath school. I continued in this place for nearly a year, teaching the little children, and preaching to a few grown persons, who would come in at times to hear what this Baptist man had to say; and who, after satisfying their curiosity, would generally leave me. During my stay in this locality, I could not find half a dozen colored Baptists, who would take hold with me in this missionary enterprise. There were some few attached to the white churches; but only two of those showed any disposition to help me in this great and good work. I found that everybody loved to go with the multitude, and it was truly up-hill work with me. I found some who are called Anti-Mission, or Old School Baptists, who, when I called upon them, would ask of what faith I was,-- and when I would reply, that I belonged to what I understood to be the Regular Baptists, they would answer, "Then you are not of our faith," &c.

Now I felt lonely indeed, separated far from home, from family, from dear brethren and friends; thrown among strangers in a strange place. Those I came to benefit, stood aloof from me, and seemed to look upon all my movements with distrust and suspicion, and opposed to all I was trying to do for the moral and spiritual benefit of our degraded race. But, thanks be to God, all I found in Baltimore were not of this stamp. Those of the white Baptists who had been the means of calling me to this field, adhered to me like brethren, indeed. Could I feel at liberty to mention names, I would bring to notice some dear friends who have ever stood by me, in all my efforts to do good, and whose acts of disinterested benevolence have been rarely equaled. But their labors of love are recorded on high, and I must forbear.

CHAPTER V.

Experience in Baltimore--Education--
Purchase of a Wife and Two Children--
Great Distress of Mind--Generous
Assistance--Church Matters.

WHEN I came among the colored people of Baltimore, I found, to my surprise, that they were advanced in education, quite beyond what I had conceived of. Of course, as I never had such advantages, I was far behind the people; and as this did not appear well in a preacher, I felt very small, when comparing my abilities with others of a superior stamp. I found that the great mass of colored professors of religion were Methodists, whose piety and zeal seemed to carry all before them. There were, at that time, some ten or eleven colored Methodist churches, one Episcopalian, one Presbyterian; and one little Baptist church, located upon the outskirts of the city. The most of the Methodist churches were large and influential; and the Presbyterian church had one of the best Sabbath schools for colored children in the city.

But the Baptist colored membership was looked upon as the smallest; and under these circumstances, I was surrounded with discouragements; although the ministers and brethren of other denominations have always treated me with marked Christian kindness.

I had never had a day's schooling; and coming to one of the first cities in the Union, where the colored people had the advantages of schools, and where their pulpits were occupied, Sabbath after Sabbath, by comparatively intelligent colored ministers-- what could I expect, but that the people would turn away from one who was trying to preach in the room of a private house, some fifteen by twenty feet? Yet, there was no turning back: God had called me to the work, and it was His cause I was advocating.

I found, that to preach, like other preachers, I must improve my mind, by reading the Bible and other good books, and by studying my own language. I started afresh--I got a small stock of books, and the white brethren loaned and gave me other useful volumes, to which they added a word of instruction and encouragement, whenever an opportunity offered; and the ministers cordially invited me to attend their Monday ministerial conference meeting, which was very useful to me.

* * I had now been in Baltimore more than a year. My wife and seven children were still in Virginia. I went to see them as often as my circumstances permitted--three or four times a year. About this time, my wife's mistress agreed to sell to me my wife and our two youngest children. The price fixed, was eight hundred dollars cash, and she gave me twelve months to raise the money. The sun rose bright in my sky that day; but before the year was out, my prospects were again in darkness. Now I had two great burdens upon my mind: one to attend properly to my missionary duty, the other to raise eight hundred dollars. During this time we succeeded in getting a better place for the Sabbath school, and there was a larger attendance upon my preaching, which demanded reading and study, and also visiting, and increased my daily labors. On

the other hand, the year was running away, in which I had to raise eight hundred dollars. So that I found myself at times in a great strait.

My plan to raise the money was, to secure the amount, first, by pledges, before I collected any. * * Finally, the year was more than passed away, and I had upon my subscription list about one-half of the money needed. It was now considered that the children had increased in value one hundred dollars, and I was told that I could have them, by paying in cash six hundred dollars, and giving a bond, with good security, for three hundred more, payable in twelve months. I had six weeks, in which to consummate this matter. I felt deeply, that this was a time to pray the Lord to help me, and for this, my wife's prayers were fervently offered with my own. I had left my wife in Virginia, and come to Baltimore, a distance of over a hundred miles; I had been separated thus for nearly three years; I had been trying to make arrangements to have her with me, for over twelve months, and as yet had failed. We were oppressed with the most gloomy forebodings, and could only kneel down together and pray for God's direction and help.

I was in Fredericksburg, and had but one day longer to stay, and spend with my wife. What could be done, must be done quickly. I went to my old friend, Mr. Wright, and stated my case to him. After hearing of all I had done, and the conditions I had to comply with, he told me that if I would raise the six hundred dollars cash, he would endorse my bond for the remaining three hundred.-- This promise inspired me with new life. The next thing was, how could the six hundred dollars be obtained in six weeks. I had upon my subscription list and in pledges nearly four hundred dollars. But this had to be collected from friends living in Fredericksburg, Washington city, Baltimore, and Philadelphia.

I left Fredericksburg, and spent a few days in Washington, to collect what I could of the money promised to me there; and met much encouragement, several friends doubling their subscriptions. When I arrived in Baltimore, and made known the peculiar strait I was in, to my joyful surprise, some of the friends who had pledged five dollars, gave me ten; and one dear friend who had promised me ten dollars, for this object, and who had previously contributed largely in the purchase of myself, now gave me fifty. I began to count up, and in two weeks from the time I commenced collecting, I had in hand four hundred dollars. Presently, another very dear friend enquired of me how I was getting along; and when I told him, he said, "Bring your money to me." I did so. It lacked two hundred dollars to make the purchase. This, the best friend I ever had in the world, made up the six hundred dollars, and said, "Go, get your wife; and you can keep on collecting, and repay the two hundred dollars when you get able."

I was now overcome with, gratitude and joy, and knew not what to say; and when I began to speak, he would not have any of my thanks. I went to my boarding house, and shut myself up in my room, where I might give vent to the gratitude of my heart: and, O, what a melting time I had! It was to me a day of thanksgiving.

Having now in band the six hundred dollars, and the promise of Mr. Wright's security for three hundred more, I was, by twelve o'clock, next day in Fredericksburg.

At first sight, my wife was surprised that I had come back so soon; for it was only two weeks since I had left her; and when I informed her that I had come after her and the children, she could hardly believe me. In a few days, having duly arranged all things relative to the purchase and removal, we left for Baltimore, with feelings commingled with joy and sorrow-- at parting with five of our older children, and our many friends; and rejoicing in the prospect of remaining together permanently in the missionary field, where God had called me to labor. I arrived in Baltimore, with my wife and two little ones, November 5th, 1851, and stopped with sister Hester Ann Hughes, a worthy member of the M. E. Church, with whom I had been boarding for four years.

The Md. Baptist Union Association was now in session here, and it became my duty to prepare my church letter and missionary report, for that body. The church had now been organized just three years; commencing with only four members, including the pastor. Our church statistics for the year, as reported, were: Baptized, 2; Received by letter, 2; Present number of members, 15 . . . . . . Sabbath school much revived, under the special efforts of several white brethren and sisters. Present number of Sunday scholars, 50.

This year was a joyful one to me--my little church increasing, and the Sabbath school flourishing, under the superintendence of the late truly excellent brother James C. Crane, though he was with us but for a short season. My wife and little ones were also with me, both in the church and Sabbath school. I was a happy man, and felt more than ever inclined to give thanks to God, and serve Him to the best of my ability.

My salary was only three hundred dollars a year; but with hard exertion and close economy, together with my wife's taking in washing and going out at day's work, we were enabled by the first of the year, to pay the two hundred dollars our dear friend had loaned us, in raising, the six hundred dollars before spoken of. But the bond for three hundred dollars was now due, and how must this be met? I studied out a plan; which was to get some gentleman who might want a little servant girl, to take my child, and advance me three hundred dollars for the purpose of paying my note, which was now due in Virginia. In this plan, I succeeded; and had my own life insured for seven years for five hundred dollars, and made it over to this gentleman, as security; until I ultimately paid him the whole amount; though I was several years in paying it.

Among the number that joined our little church, was a young brother, Jos. M. Harden, who was baptized by Dr. Fuller, but soon became a valuable member with us, both in the church and Sunday school. He was born in Baltimore, and had been early taught to read, and though he had been at ten years old bound out, till he was twenty-one, his love of books had made him far superior to colored people generally, and he was very valuable to me. Things had gone on hopefully with me, and my little church, though our progress was very slow. But we had to suffer a loss in brother Harden's leaving us for the great missionary field in Africa, where I trust the Lord has sent him for a great and happy work. But God has blessed us in the person of brother Samuel W. Madden, whose labors as a licensed preacher for several years have been invaluable to us.

CHAPTER VI.

A New Movement in Baltimore--Erection of a Meeting House for the African Baptist Church--Heavy Indebtedness --Account of the Enterprise--Personal Troubles.

FOR several years previous to Jan., 1855, our little church and Sunday school had occupied a very inconvenient upper room on Courtland street. Our particular friend, Mr. William Crane, with some other white persons to aid him, was the devoted superintendent of our Sunday school, and the unfailing friend of our own little church, as well as of me personally. Mr. Crane had felt, with us, the great disadvantage of our place of worship, and had exerted himself much to obtain a more commodious room for us. But in July, 1853; he commenced an extraordinary effort in our behalf, by purchasing a lot-- one hundred feet by forty-six feet--with three fronts, on Calvert, Saratoga and Davis streets, on which a chapel building has been erected for us.

Our chapel was opened for worship Feb. 18, 1855; and Rev. Dr. Fuller preached the opening sermon to a crowded audience.

On this occasion Mr. Wm. Crane read a detailed report of all the facts relative to this building--a full copy of this report may be interesting probably to my readers, and I have therefore obtained it, and here present it, in connection with a picture of the building, which will be found opposite the title page.

HISTORY OF THE SARATOGA STREET AFRICAN BAPTIST CHAPEL.

"THE questions have often been asked in this vicinity during the last six months, Who is putting up that large building called the 'Saratoga Street African Baptist Chapel?' 'What are they putting it up for?'-- 'Who will own it, when finished?' 'How much will it cost? and who will pay for it?'

These questions have often been answered, but it seems proper, and indeed necessary, at this time to answer them plainly and clearly, for the information of this large assembly.

First, then, I reply: This, entire building has been reared under my directions, in the name of the Saratoga street African Baptist Church.

This Church was organized with only four members, six years ago, with brother Noah Davis, a missionary of the Md. Baptist Union Association, as its pastor, who has labored post faithfully in his work. But, although colored churches of the Baptist denomination in all of our Southern and Western cities count their members by thousands, this church has now only thirty members--but our hope and prayer is, that established here in the center of a population of full thirty thousand colored people, God may bless the humble devoted efforts of His people, and increase their numbers a hundred fold. Four years ago, the 1st of January, we commenced a Sunday school in Courtland street,--where this church has always held its regular meetings, which notwithstanding its many discouragements--mostly from a want of devoted self-denying teachers--has been unremittingly kept up morning and afternoon, till the present time, with an attendance varying from thirty to over one hundred scholars; and we feel assured that the hundreds of Bibles and Testaments, tracts, &c., with the Sunday school instructions, and the preaching of brother Davis will have laid the foundation for a lasting blessing to his people This little church and Sunday school have met to-day for the first time in this building, and in the language of the Psalmist David, probably on an occasion like this, we would exclaim, "Send now, we beseech thee, O Lord--O Lord, we beseech thee, send now Prosperity!"--(Ps. 118: 25.)

But what are the objects for which this house has been built? I answer, the first object was, to furnish such a room as this, for the use of this church, where the gospel might be preached and its ordinances administered, and where Sunday schools and religious associations might be properly accommodated. The second was, to furnish rooms in the next story, for a male high school at one end, and a female high school at the other, and where colored missionaries for Africa might be educated for that most important field of labor; with a large hall in the center, for a lecture room, or for any other religious, moral, or useful purposes. The upper story has four separate rooms, finished for renting to associations of colored people, with a view to paying whatever debt may remain on the building, and for defraying its current expenses; --and it is hoped that, at some future day, a reading room and a circulating library for colored people may also be located here--the whole of it combining a most respectable, central, commodious Colored People's Home.

But it is asked, who owns this building? I admit that it is an unusually mixed up affair; but I will try to explain it. After a great deal of searching and enquiring after a lot or building, where this Church and Sunday school could have a settled home, about two years ago, I was I informed that this lot was for sale; and realizing instantly that my cherished objects could here be accomplished I bought it without hesitation, for five thousand dollars; but the loss of two years' interest and the amount paid to tenants to move away, makes the cost of the lot now full six thousand dollars. I obtained the deed of J.H.B. Latrobe, Esq., who sold it, as trustee for the estate of Hugh Finley, deceased, under an order of Court. After a charter of incorporation for the Church had been made, I got Mr. Latrobe to draw up also this deed, [here presenting it] which he says is a perfectly good one--from William Crane and wife, to Geo. F. Adams, J. W. M.

Williams, and John W. Ball, as trustees for all concerned, conveying to this Church all my right and title forever to all of the proposed building on this lot above the. first story: leaving me the basement and the cellar as my own property forever with the proviso, that the Church in its own name should put up the entire building. But I agreed at the same time to subscribe five thousand dollars on the subscription book of the Church towards erecting it. So that I am now sole owner of the store and cellar under the Chapel--the Church has no ownership there at all--but the Church is legal, owner of this Chapel and all the rooms above it. The Church appointed me their agent to build the house, and as, such I have made all the contracts, paid out all the monies, and assumed all the liabilities. Before commencing the building, as before stated, my own subscription was $5,000

- My brother, J. C. Crane, from whom I expected efficient personal aid, gave . .1,000
- Bro. Franklin, Wilson, ... 1,000
- A. Fuller Crane, ... 500

- John W. Ball, ... 250
- J. B. Thomas, ... 100
- Among our colored friends, about 200
- Amounting to, say, ... $8,050

Since that time, the pressure on the money market has prevented any general effort to obtain subscriptions, but a city pastor has subscribed $150

- A sister of the First Baptist Church 100
- Bro. Jonathan Batchelor, of Lynn, Mass . . . 100
- Making in all, a total of $8,400

The entire cost of the building, notwithstanding the most rigid economy, will be over eighteen thousand dollars, and full half of this amount is yet unprovided for. The bills are not all presented, but some of the larger ones which have been settled by notes will be due in a short time; while the largest one, the lumber bill, has six months to run yet, so that I am bound to settle up and pay the entire balance of expenditure on this house, as agent of the

Church, within the coming six months. And whatever amount of money I advance over and above the subscriptions and collections must, of course, remain as a debt due me by the Church, and be on interest until paid.

The last question, how is the money obtained to pay for the building? has been partly answered; but a full explanation of it will depend on what the friends of the object will now contribute toward paying for it. I will subscribe one dollar for every ten dollars that may be subscribed and paid on account of the Church debt within the year 1855. In other words, I will add ten per cent to any amount, which may be contributed. I may remark, that in engaging in this project, I had not a dollar, which I wished to put out at interest. I want much more than my capital in my mercantile business. I am in fact borrowing, to lend to the Church. But it is God's cause, and I have had to trust in Him to bear me through it. The failing health of my dear brother, J. C. Crane,* and the want of his invaluable cooperation with me, as well as the lack of hearty, zealous assistance on the part of many other brethren and friends, has been painful to me. But I hope, now that the house is finished, the friends of our Redeemer's cause and of the African race generally, may not fail in lending their efficient aid.

I have only to add, brethren, "the time is short;" we must all of us soon appear before the judgment seat of Christ, to render an account
* Died March 31 1857 See Memoir of Southern Baptist Publication Society of all the talents committed to our charge. If God has given me a talent for the acquisition of money over and above what my duty to my family requires, I regard myself bound as a good steward to exert that talent entirely for Him. I am not my own, and I feel perfectly assured that any individual who possesses the tact and ability for acquiring money is necessarily the best qualified for a judicious and proper disbursement of it; and I dare not try to leave my earthly acquisitions in testamentary charitable bequests--to the inexperienced and uncertain management of those who may come after me.

May God help us to work for Him, and at last may we hear, 'Well done, good and faithful servant; enter thou into the joy of thy Lord.'"

This paper was read to the congregation, probably a thousand people, immediately after Dr. Fuller had preached the opening sermon, Feb, 18, 1855; and a collection was taken of about one hundred dollars. Subsequent to this, a venerable widow lady of Baltimore contributed $500, and other quite liberal donations were made.

On the 1st of July, 1855, Mr. Crane rendered a full account to the Church and trustees, of all the monies received and bills paid on the building; showing that the entire cost of it was, ... $18,207,73
Total am't of collections credited, . . .9,547,86
Leaving balance over-paid by him, . . $8,659,87

The trustees then gave Mr. Crane a bond for this balance, and a lease on the building, until this debt, with interest on it, could be paid.

Our Church now had great cause of gratitude at finding ourselves in a fine large Chapel, in the center of our city--a room 100 feet long, and 19 feet high, with a gallery at each end, a baptistery, gas lights, and sliding partitions, to make two closed rooms under the galleries, when needed for the changing of clothes on baptismal occasions, as well as for our Church prayer and conference meetings.

We were in hopes that we could rent out the large hall, together with the six other spacious rooms in the two upper stories, for schools, benevolent societies, &c., so as to pay the interest on our debt, if no more; but so far, we have not been able to do this. My own trials , with my family, have greatly retarded my efforts in this matter. We have had the largest and best weekday school for colored children in the city--a part of the time with three teachers and over one hundred scholars--but for four years, no rent has been received from the school. The prices for tuition have been so low, that they have hardly sustained the teachers; but we trust that our people have derived much benefit from them already, and hope they may receive much more good from them in the future. Since the dedication of our Chapel, our Church has more than doubled its membership, and the congregation has increased four-fold; while on our baptizing occasions the hall is generally full. We have always held three meetings for worship every Sunday, to accommodate many servants, who have no command of their time, and also regular Wednesday and Friday evening prayer and conference meetings. Our Sunday school has always had two sessions a day--an hour and a half in the morning, and an hour in the afternoon.

I have been necessarily much hindered in my own labors, from pecuniary embarrassments, arising from the sale of my children, who were left in Virginia--two daughters and three sons. The first of these, who was about to be sold, and taken away South, was my oldest daughter; and it was with great difficulty and the help of friends that I raised eight hundred and fifty dollars, and got her on to Baltimore. But I was soon called upon to make a similar effort to save my eldest son from being sold far from me. Entirely unexpected, I received the painful news that my boy was in one of the trader's jails in Richmond, and for sale. The dealer knew me, and was disposed to let me have him, if I could get anyone to purchase him. I was, of course, deeply anxious to help my boy; but I began to think that I had already drawn so heavily on the liberality of all my friends, that to appeal to them again seemed out of the question. I immediately wrote to the owners of my son, and received an answer--that his price was fixed at seven hundred dollars.

The fact is, God had already done so much more for me and my family than we had ever expected that we could not tell what further help He might give us, until we had asked Him for it; and we could but pray over this trying affair. I hardly knew what else to do, but pray. The boy was twenty years old, and had been I accustomed to waiting in the house, for the most respectable families. It occurred to me, that I might perhaps get him a home near me, where we might see him and use our parental influence over him. I thought it was possible, that I might find three hundred persons among my friends in Baltimore, who would contribute one dollar each to save my son, and that I might then obtain some friend in Baltimore to advance four hundred dollars, and let my son work it out with him: and give this friend a life insurance policy on the boy, as a security. This plan seemed practicable, and I wrote to his owners, asking for ten days to raise the money; which they granted me.

I now got my case made known publicly to the different colored congregations in the city --and was very much surprised to find how many friends I had, and how kindly they engaged in helping me. The result of it was, that I obtained the three hundred dollars, and also a kind friend to advance the four hundred dollars, within the ten days, and recovered my son; who is now doing well, in working out the money advanced on him.

So far, I felt that I had great reason to say, "Hitherto the Lord hath helped me." I had obtained my own freedom and also that of my wife and four children.

But three of my children were still in bondage. In 1856, the mistress of these remaining ones died; and in settling up her estate, it became necessary to sell all her servants at auction with her other property. This was the decision of the Court; and commissioners were appointed to carry out the sale, on the 1st of January, 1857. I felt now, that I had gone as far as I could in getting my family free; for I felt very certain that my daughter, about whom I felt the greatest anxiety, would sell at auction for more money than I could get any of my friends in Baltimore to give for her; and I saw no way to do anything for the two boys. I thought I had no chance of raising any more money myself, and I could only pray the Lord to grant no His grace, to reconcile us and the children, to whatever might come upon us. But before the end of the year, when the sale was to take place, the time was extended six months by the Court. My hopes now began to revive again; I began to think that if I could be at the sale, my daughter, though a grown up girl might possibly not bring over six or seven hundred dollars. In that case, I might perhaps get six or twelve months' time, and get some friend in Baltimore to help me, as had been the case with my son. The sale was postponed for six months longer, and finally occurred, Jan. 1, 1858.

The money panic, of 1857, had partially destroyed my hopes of doing anything to relieve my daughter;--But I had secured the promise of a kind friend in Baltimore, to go to Fredericksburg with me, and if he liked the appearance of the boys, to buy one or both of them. But in this, I was disappointed; for on the day of sale this gentleman was confined to his house by sickness. The sale went on. My oldest son, aged twenty-one, sold for $560; and the younger one, just turning his seventeenth year, brought $570. They were bought in by their young master. But my daughter was run up to $990, by a slave trader, who after the sale agreed to let my friends have her, for me, for eleven hundred dollars. These friends were gentlemen of the first standing in the place, who, out of kindness to me, whom they had well known for years, gave their bond jointly for the amount, and in this case again I got the girl's life insured for one thousand dollars as a security for them. The girl was of course left in the hands of these gentlemen, in, whom I had the most implicit confidence.

I returned to Baltimore, and prepared for the redemption of my child. I had a circular printed, showing the facts as they were, and scattered it among my friends.

CHAPTER VII.

Account of a Visit to the northern Cities--
True Friends.

During the winter and spring, I used every effort in my power in the way of collecting funds, but, though I met with the most generous sympathy and kindness from all my friends--up to the 1st of June I had in hand only one hundred and fifty dollars. I then applied to the Mission Board for permission to travel and solicit funds to help me out of my distress. This was readily granted me. Having obtained a certificate, relative to the objects of my journey, signed by Rev. Franklin Wilson, Secretary of our State Missionary Board, as well as by the pastors and other friends in Baltimore, I started once more on this painful business of begging money, to purchase my fifth child out of slavery. I went to Philadelphia, and met with marked attention from the ministers of the Baptist churches generally, and especially from Rev. Messrs. McKean, Cole, and Griffith, with whom I had been acquainted in Baltimore; as well, as Revs. Messrs Cuthbert and Malcom, and the editors of the Christian Chronicle, Presbyterian, &c. I obtained in this city nearly two hundred dollars.

With a view to meet a particular friend in Boston, I was induced to visit that city next. The many acts of kindness and sympathy I met with there can never be effaced from my memory. I had a special introduction to the Messrs., Gould and Lincoln, book publishers. To the latter, I owe a lasting obligation.-- Through him I obtained a hearing of my case in Mr. Anderson's church, Roxbury, where I obtained very liberal aid, while the pastor was absent, as well as in many other cases.

I called on Rev. Dr. Stow, who allowed my case to be presented to his congregation, at an evening meeting, where I received some fifty dollars. He also gave me a letter of commendation to the other Baptist ministers, with a request that they would also sign it, which a large number did. The article was then published gratuitously for me in the "Watchman, and Reflector" and "Christian Era," Rev. L.A. Grimes, pastor of the 12th Baptist Church, (colored,) from the respectable position which he occupied in the community, did much for me, in furthering my cause, and, introducing me to others, especially at the daily prayer meetings.

I had the great privilege and pleasure of mingling with the people of God of every name, in these blessed meetings. The first I went to, was at the old South Chapel. Here I felt at first greatly embarrassed when called on to speak or pray. I thought that those who came to these meetings must be among the most pious and intelligent people in Boston. The kind manner in which they treated me, confirmed me in my impressions of them. But the best meetings, I think I ever enjoyed on earth, for such a length of time, (nearly two months,) was at what was called the North street prayer meeting, or Father Mason's. This was in a large upper room. It really appeared to me, that the most of those who met at this place each day at twelve o'clock to spend an hour in prayer, to tell what God had done for their souls, bad been made "ready," by the Spirit of God before they reached that sacred spot.--

I know I shall fail to present a true picture of this heavenly place; for such it was to me, and many others. But, it may be, that my own peculiar circumstances may have rendered the meetings unusually precious to me. But they were good to me in many respects. I was a poor colored man, in distress, and needed Christian sympathy. I found it truly, among the many white friends with whom I met in the North street prayer meeting. There, in that meeting, the dear friends would pray with me and for me. In a word, I felt at times it was good for me to be afflicted, for surely, if it bad not been for my peculiar circumstances, I should never have been inside the Old South Chapel, or North street prayer meeting, where I enjoyed so much of God's presence, and found so many real friends, in the midst of strangers. I felt that I realized what the apostle Peter meant: "If need be, ye are in heaviness, through manifold temptation, that the trials of your faith, being much more precious than gold that perisheth, though it be tried with fire, might be found unto praise and honor and glory, at the appearing of Jesus Christ." --(1 Peter 1: 6,7.) Also, "For I will show him how great things he must suffer for my name's sake."--(Acts 9: 16.) The arguments I drew from these passages of Scripture were, to show that when God wanted to purify our faith, and strengthen our confidence in Him, He would send trials upon us. And to let us see how great the things we must suffer for His name's sake, and to let us see too how great the grace He gives us, to enable us to endure hardness, as good soldiers of the cross.

Suffice it to say, the friends in Boston and its vicinity gave me about four hundred dollars towards the purchase of my daughter. I had the privilege of meeting the Baptist ministers in their conference meeting. Here the Rev. Mr. Tilson, pastor of the First Baptist Church at Hingham, invited we to spend a Sunday evening at his place, which I did, very greatly to my own satisfaction and profit. During my stay in Boston, I visited several of the smaller towns adjacent to it,-- Lynn, Cambridge,

Melrose, Malden, Chelsea, and others, and I was kindly received at all of them. I collected in Lynn something like $50, the most of which was given to me by the members of the 2nd Baptist Church. Just before leaving Boston, to my great and agreeable surprise, I met Dr. F. Patten, surgeon in the U.S. Navy, (my former owner,) in the street, in that city. I had not seen him for seven or eight years, and had no thought of seeing him in Boston. He recognized me first, and spoke to me before I knew he was near; but I instantly knew him. We greeted each other heartily, and he invited me to visit him at Chelsea. This I did, the same afternoon, and was kindly treated.

While I sat there with him and his children, and he was looking over my subscription book, I was constrained to look back for fifteen years, over all the way the Lord had brought me, since the day this same gentleman had given me privilege to purchase my freedom, and handed me a pass, saying, "I am not afraid of you running away, Noah-- you may go where you please." I reflected, suppose I had stayed away, when I was in Boston, twelve years ago, begging money to buy myself--how would it be with me and my family to-day? But I have tried to acknowledge the Lord in all my ways, always asking counsel of Him, and I now feel that He has kindly directed and kept me.

I also visited New Bedford, where I met a large number of my old acquaintances from Virginia, and had the privilege of presenting my object to several of the Churches, and I received in all about $50. I next went to Providence, Rhode Island, where I spent a couple of weeks greatly to my advantage. It was indeed "providence" to me. I was permitted to present my case to nearly all the Baptist Churches in that city. Five of these aided my cause; but their great kindness deserves some particular notice. The first one I visited was Rev. Mr. Stone's, whose congregation, with himself, greatly encouraged me. At the First Church I told my story before an evening meeting, and shall never forget the kindness of the pastor, the senior deacon, and others. I obtained here nearly $100. I was kindly assisted by Rev. Mr. Keyser's Church, also the Fourth Baptist Church. But at the Central Baptist Church, Rev. Mt. Fields', I found unbounded kindness and liberality. After seeing my letters of recommendation, the pastor invited me to his prayer meeting, where I was favored with the privilege of telling my story, freely. I had been from home several months, and had collected in all about seven hundred dollars, but still lacked about four hundred to accomplish my object. I was receiving letters every week from my Church and family, saying that my presence at home was greatly needed; but the idea of going home without accomplishing my great object, filled me with distress. While speaking to the meeting, and telling how God had delivered me from time to time out of trials, I felt such a sense of my condition, that for the moment I could not restrain my feelings --my heart became so full, that it stopped all utterance. At the close of the meeting, the people showed their sympathy for me by giving me a collection of sixty one dollars.--One dear brother, (may the Lord bless him!) came forward, and presenting me with a ten dollar bill, said, "Brother Davis, give yourself no more trouble about that daughter.-- You say you have to stop in New York. Let me say, that when you get home, whatever you lack of the four hundred dollars, write to me, and I will send you a check for the balance." This was spoken in the presence of the whole meeting. I felt completely at a loss for words of gratitude and thanksgiving and merely said, the day is broke, and the Lord has appeared for me indeed!

I now left Providence, feeling in my heart that the place is rightly called by that name, as far as I am concerned.

I then went to New York. In that great city, I met with considerable assistance. I never started out, but it seemed that the Lord directed my steps. I was allowed to address a prayer meeting of the First Baptist Church, whose pastor was the late excellent Rev. A.K. Nott, and was aided to the amount of over seventy dollars.

Rev. Dr. Lathrop, with much Christian kindness, invited me to his night meeting;

but a severe rain prevented any attendance. He invited me again, and then he was absent because of illness. I was depressed with disappointment; but he had sent a request that I might be heard, (as I afterward learned,) and I was called on to state my case to the audience. I was taken by surprise, for the pastor's illness had taken all hope from me of accomplishing anything there. Still I begun, by telling my experience. I said that when it had pleased God to convert my soul, I thought that all my trouble was gone, and gone forever; but I had since learned that I was much mistaken--I had learned that "in the world we shall have tribulation." I then went on to state my present trouble and distress--and before I left the meeting, I received with heart-felt gratitude, one hundred and thirty four dollars, This reminded me of Providence.

Rev. Drs. Gillette and Armitage treated me with much generous sympathy, as also did many others.

I visited Greenport on Long Island, where Rev. Henry Knapp kindly aided me.

Elders Swan and Read, and the brethren generally at New London, aided me to the amount of about fifty dollars.

CHAPTER VIII.
Conclusion--Object of this Book.

I NOW left the north, for home, and arrived there safely. My friends greeted me cordially on my success in collecting money.

I still lacked, however, one hundred and forty-two dollars of the needed eleven hundred. I had used every effort in my power to prevent the necessity of having to call on my generous friend in Providence. But in spite of all my endeavors, I had to make known to him this deficiency, which he immediately and generously supplied, by remitting me a check for the full amount.

I was now prepared to go after my daughter, which I did, December 1st, 1858; thus releasing her within one year from the time she was sold. She is now with me, and doing well.

I received a promise from the young master of my two sons, at the time he purchased them, that if I should succeed in paying for my daughter during that year, he would let me know what I might have my two boys for. At the time, my boys were about returning to Richmond, where they had been hired out for several years. I charged them to let me hear a good report of their conduct; and if I could do anything for them, after I had got through with the purchase of their sister, I would do it. This. pledge I made to the boys, in the presence of their master's agent.

Having, through the aid of a kind Providence, been enabled to pay for my daughter, I have felt it my duty to turn my attention toward redeeming my word to my last children now in bondage.

But this, of course, has called up anxious thought and prayerful meditation. I have also considered the peculiar condition of my church--the large outlay of money in the erection of the building, and the heavy debt hanging upon it, which is increased every year by the interest. I have also considered how long I have been supported in this field of labor by the Missionary Board of the Southern Baptist Convention and the Maryland Baptist Union Association.

The question then occurred to me, Could I not, by making a book, do something to relieve myself and my children, and ultimately, by the same means, help my church, under its heavy debt, and also relieve the Missionary Board from helping me. This idea struck me with so, much force, that I have yielded to it--that is, to write a short Narrative of my own life, setting forth the trials and difficulties the Lord has brought me through to this day, and offer it for sale to my friends generally, as well as to the public at large; and, I hope it may not only aid me, but may serve to encourage others, who meet with similar difficulties, to put their trust in God.

END OF THE NARRATIVE.

SERMON.

SERMON.

BY REV. NOAH DAVIS

TEXT.--"But if any provide not for his own, and especially for those of his own house, he hath denied the faith, and is worse than an infidel."--1 Tim. 5: 8.

IN this chapter, we have several Christian duties set forth by the apostle Paul, to Timothy, a young preacher of the gospel, who was to teach other Christians to observe them, as evidences of the genuineness of their faith in Christ.

That faith which does not produce obedience to the commands of Jesus must be regarded as defective. Religion requires us to love God, and all men, and we must show our faith, by a life consistent with our profession.

If human nature, fallen as it is, prompts men of the world to labor zealously to supply their own temporal necessities and the wants of those whom Providence has made to depend upon them, how much more will it be expected of those who profess to have drank of that pure Fountain of love, the Spirit of our blessed Lord and Savior, Jesus Christ. God has indeed doomed man to eat his bread in the sweat of his face; but as if to reward him, he has connected with it a pleasure in the labor, and especially, in our efforts to do good to others.

In speaking from these words, let us first consider what is here meant by "providing" for "his own;" secondly, "and especially for those of his own house;" thirdly, what it is to "deny the faith;" and lastly, draw a comparison between the one who "hath denied the faith" and the "infidel."

1. In the first place, we are to consider the duty enjoined in the text, to provide for our own: which we understand to mean our own temporal wants, such as food and raiment and every temporal benefit. Every man is bound by the laws of nature to provide for himself the necessaries of life, honestly in the sight of God and men, as far as in him lieth. This both reason and common sense dictate. This religion

inspires. "He that will not work, shall not eat," is the teaching of the Word of God. "Provide things honest in the sight of all men," is the instruction of the great apostle to the Gentiles; at the same time giving them an example, by working with his own hands, to supply his necessities, and the wants of those who were with him. I have heard it said that a lazy person cannot be a Christian, and the same idea seems to be supported in my text.

"But if any provide not for his own." Religion benefits those who possess it, by regulating their appetite for temporal things, as well as giving them a relish for spiritual ones. While we are in love with sin, we labor hard to enjoy its pleasures. How industriously do wicked men labor for what they can eat, drink and wear. And shall a Christian be less active to secure for himself the necessaries of life?--he would prove himself indeed to be worse than the infidel. But we have other wants to be supplied, beside those of the body. God has given to all men an intellectual nature--a mind, which distinguishes them from the brutes. These minds are capable of improvement; and every man is under obligation to make use of the means and opportunities which God has given him for cultivating his mind, by educating himself, that he may be useful to himself and those around him. But man is a social being as well as an intellectual one. "God hath made of one blood, all nations of men, for to dwell on all the face of the earth.-- (Acts 17: 26.) Much of our happiness, and usefulness in this world arises from this quality which man possesses over the animal creation. And just in proportion, as we shall cultivate, and refine our social and intellectual natures, just in that proportion, shall we rise above the level of the savage and the heathen.

But man has a soul, which must be fitted for the enjoyment of God, here and hereafter. Now to provide for the wants of the soul, is our highest duty on earth.--Sin has unclothed us of that innocence in which our Creator first made us, and the responsibility now rests upon every soul, to provide a clothing which will stand the inspection of God himself. This clothing,

Christ has prepared through His sufferings, and death, and it is given to all them that believe in Him. And surely, if it be our duty to provide temporal things for ourselves, and for those of our own house, how much more are we bound to seek and secure the one thing needful.

2. But we will consider in the second place, what is meant by providing for our own house?--"and especially for those of his own house?" House here means family. First, we will consider the duty devolving upon a Christian parent, in making suitable provision for his own house, or family. This embraces all we have urged as his duty to himself. It is the duty of all parents, to provide for their families every temporal good which adds to their own comfort or usefulness in life. And it is no less the duty of parents to provide for the spiritual necessities of their own families. And first-- we shall consider the duty of parents, to provide suitable training for their children. This is a duty which God has enjoined and approves. He said of Abraham, "For I know him, that he will command his children and

his household after him, and they shall keep the way of the Lord, to do justice and judgment, that the Lord may bring upon Abraham, that which He hath spoken of him." The duty of parents to train their children religiously, is clearly taught under the gospel dispensation.

"And ye fathers, provoke not your children to wrath, but bring them up in the nurture and admonition of the Lord." Here, we have divine authority, for teaching our children, the things, which make for their good, both in this life and that which is to come. But it may be asked, to what extent are parents bound to comply with these high and solemn obligations? We answer, to the utmost of their ability. To whom much is given, of him much is required, and to whom little is given, of him little is required.-- But all are bound to train up their children "in the way they should go, that when they are old, they may not depart from it." This duty is seen in the judgments which God has visited upon those parents and children who have neglected to obey the Lord in this particular.--(1 Samuel 2: 34.)

3. We are, in the third place, to enquire what it is to "deny the faith." Much is said in the Scriptures about faith. Much depends upon it. We are said to be "justified by faith," and "saved by faith;" we "live by faith." And inasmuch, as such as are spoken of in the text are said to be worse than an infidel, because they provide not for themselves and families, thereby showing that they have denied the faith, therefore let us try to consider what genuine faith is, and what it is to deny it. This is the most important point in the subject now before us. "Without faith it is impossible to please God."

We will consider some of the effects of this distinguishing grace. There are several kinds of faith spoken of in the Bible. In one case, men are said to "believe for a while." This faith is shown us in the parable taught by our blessed Savior, in the characters represented by the seed sown upon the rock, "which for a while believe, and in time of temptation fall away."--(Luke 8: 33.)

There is a faith which is called dead.--"Even so faith, if it hath not works, is dead, being alone."--(James 2: 17.) But the faith which enables the Christian to obey the Savior in all things, is said to "work by love." --(Gal. 5: 6.) Now we say that those who have this faith, will never deny it. The counterfeit may deceive, but the genuine cannot. We say this faith cannot deny itself. All who are spoken of in the Old Testament as having this faith never denied it. By it Abel made a more excellent sacrifice to God than Cain. By it, Enoch walked with God, when the other portion of mankind walked in the vain wicked imaginations of their own hearts. "By faith Noah, being warned of God of things not seen as yet, moved with fear, prepared an ark for the saving of his house." "Abraham believed God, and it was counted unto him for righteousness."

This is the grace which enables believers to renounce the pleasures of sin, which are but for a season. It gives them a complete victory over the world. It abideth with hope and charity. Now, whosoever professes this faith, and then by his unholy life denies it, by neglecting to provide for his own, and especially for those of his own house, makes it manifest that he never had it. It is as unchangeable as its Author, for it is the gift of God. It prompted Noah to labor over a hundred years, to build an ark, to save his house. And what it has done, it will continue to do, for those who have it. This is the principle in religion which purifies the heart, overcomes the world, and causes Christians to love one another, whatever may be their circumstances, or color or rank in life.

4. We are now in the fourth and last place to draw a comparison between those who deny the faith, and an infidel. Now an infidel, is an unbeliever in the religion of Christ.-- Yet he provides for his own, and especially for those of his own house. In this he is consistent with himself. Here he acts from reason, and principles of nature. But the individual who denies the faith, is one, who has taken upon himself the solemn vow before God and men, that he will act out what his profession supposes him to be in possession of, which is superior in its

influence, to the infidel's principles, yet he fails to do as much.

But again, an infidel is a bad man, and makes no pretensions to hide it. But he who contradicts his profession, by denying it in the manner here set forth, is worse for attempting to cover up a character, which in itself is no better. But consider the effect produced by a false faith, (and we have shown, that such a faith, as does not come up with the infidel's, is false,) it does the greatest harm. Many persons, when they make a profession of faith, suppose it is the true faith, but after a while, they find that their faith does not work by love, it does not purify their hearts. They love sin secretly, as much as before. They love worldly company as well as ever. And they find the employments, which their profession enjoins upon them, irksome and dry. Such persons are greatly deceived, yet they are ashamed to confess it, and throw off the mask of profession. And such persons are often the greatest faultfinders with those, whose true faith inspires them to endure hardness, afflictions and deny themselves and take up their cross, so that they may glorify their Savior in their bodies and spirits which are the Lord's.

In conclusion, dear brethren, let us, who have made a profession of faith, examine ourselves, whether we be in the faith of the gospel, or not. "Know ye not your own selves how that Jesus Christ is in you, except ye be reprobates." AMEN.

STATISTICAL REPORT
OF ALL THE
COLORED PROTESTANT CHURCHES
AND SABBATH SCHOOLS
IN BALTIMORE.

STATISTICAL REPORT

OF ALL THE

COLORED PROTESTANT CHURCHES
AND SABBATH SCHOOLS
IN BALTIMORE.

(As quoted from the Minutes of their respective bodies, for the year 1859.)

Sharp st. and Wesley Chapel, Meth.Ep.,	1812
Orchard st. and Asbury, "	1508
Dallas st., "	119
Bethel, Saratoga st., African M.E.,	1398
Ebenezer, Montgomery st., " "	600
Union Bethel, Fell's Point, " "	100
Water's Chapel, Spring st., " "	98
Mission " Tissia st., " "	77
South Howard st. Chapel, Zion Meth.,	200
St. Thomas', Chesnut st., Meth.Prot.,	70
St. James', Saratoga st., Episcopal,	100
Presbyterian church, Madison st.,	69
First Baptist, cor. Young and Thomson st.,	99
Union Baptist, Lewis st.,	63
Saratoga st. African Baptist Chapel,	73

Total Col'd Prot. Religious Popul'n, 6386

SABBATH SCHOOL REPORT.

(Rendered to the S. S. Union, for 1859.)

	BIBLE READS.	CONVERS'NS.	VOLS. LIBR'Y.	FEM. TEACH.	MALE TEACH.	SCHOLARS.
Sharpst., M.E.,			200	15	15	200
Orchard st., "				6	9	177
Asbury, "		2			45	259
Dallas st., "				20	17	250
John Wesley, "			250	10	10	120
Bethel, African M.E.,	60	15	200	16	16	350
Ebenezer, " "					27	178
Spring st., " "			113		13	120
Allen chapel, " "				6		58
Union Bethel, " "					11	86
Good Samaritan, "				6		60
Tissia st. " "			108		6	30
St. Thomas, M.P.,			200	3	4	56
S. How'd st., Zion,				5	7	102
Mt. Olive, Ind.,				3	7	40
Presbyterian,				20	10	240
Episcopal,			205	5	5	70
First Col'd Baptist,			78	3	3	33
Union, "					11	86
Saratoga st. "	40	1	250	8	6	150
Aggregate,	106	18	1604	126	222	2665

HISTORIC PULISHING
©2017

www.ingramcontent.com/pod-product-compliance
Lightning Source LLC
Chambersburg PA
CBHW071353090426
42738CB00012B/3110